"I've had the privilege of working with Barbara on several occasions. Her presentation, information and professionalism are of the highest quality. I would highly recommend Barbara for speaking to any group that needs a quality program on Lifestyles and Retirement Transition Coaching."
—Tisha Diffie, TMD Planning & Investment Strategies, Phoenix, AZ

"I thoroughly enjoyed the book, and at 62 -- going through a particularly rough patch -- I found that I'm actually better off than I gave myself credit for. Thank you for putting this information into a handy, assessable, inspirational form."
—Suzanne Fleming, Wayne State University, Detroit, MI

"Great workshop today, Barbara!"
—Joyce Chapman, Retired, American Express, Peoria AZ

70 is the New 40

Bonus Years Here We Come!

Barbara Atkins
9-25-15

Barbara Penn Atkins

Forward By
Dr. Damita Zweiback

Llumina
Press

Published by Llumina Press
7915 W. McNab Road
Tamarac, FL 3077-2246

Atkins, Barbara Penn
70 is the New 40: Bonus Years Here We Come
/ Barbara Penn Atkins

ISBN: 978-1-60594-356-5

Printed in the United States of America

Library of Congress Control Number: 2009909913

The purpose of this book is to provide insight regarding truths and principles for application to the reader's perceptions of aging. The information given here is designed to help you make decisions for yourself regarding how you wish to view the phases of aging. It is not intended to offer therapy or psychological counseling for personal image or emotional disturbances. Referrals to a qualified counselor or therapist are recommended for issues outside the scope of this publication, which is intended ONLY for general use and not as a specific course of treatment.

This book is dedicated to my parents,
Beatrice and Charlie Penn,
who showered me with love and
encouragement to pursue life to its
fullest, age gracefully, and
to GOD–always give the Glory.

Table of Contents

Author's Comment

Every man and woman is born into the world to do something unique and something distinctive and if he or she does not do it, it will never be done.

—Benjamin Mays

In this book, I tell my story of transitioning through the stages of my adult life, its meaning, purpose, and ultimate satisfaction. I believe my life's blessings, trials, and tribulations started at age forty. It took thirty years for me to see what God had in store for me. At age seventy, my purpose was redefined, life's meaning was illuminated, and my inner soul was filled with new joy. To all of you, particularly women age thirty and over who may think seventy is old age—think again; this book is for you! I invite you to join me on this journey as I continue to "press on toward the goal." *Philippians 3:14 (NIV)*

Foreword
by Dr. Damita J. Zweiback

We are rapidly moving into an era in which there will be more people over the age of sixty than all other age groups. Statistics show us that people are living longer and better lives. There are more than 96,500 people living in the United States over the age of one hundred. The population of centenarians is expected to increase to 601,000 by the year 2050 (Source: US Census Bureau's Public Information Office, March 2009). Reaching the age of one hundred or more is quite possible. The bonus years could represent thirty or more years of rich, new experiences and discoveries.

With that in mind, this book is right on time. Barbara Atkins has taken life by the reins, steering the direction of her bonus years on the wings of the Creator. In *70 is the New 40,* she shows us how we can do the same, no matter what age we are today, with her revolutionary way of viewing life on a new curve.

For those of you who are in your forties, read this book from cover to cover. It is a road map for living stronger and better than ever before, for making your life your own, and for owning your life. You may be at a crossroads with career decisions, or changes in family circumstances, relationships or living arrangements.

If so, *70 is the New 40* offers you inspiration, hope, and courage. It shows you a way to open yourself up to new possibilities and chart your own course.

If you're in your fifties or sixties, you might be looking forward and planning that next stage of life: retirement. There, you could be counting down the days or assessing whether you should take advantage of an early-out program if offered by your employer. On the other hand, you may be facing a layoff or pay cuts after years of service as the economy continues to slow and employers tighten their expenses to stay afloat. You may also find yourself balancing the care of aging parents and young children, making decisions for both Mom and Dad's well-being and that of your children's. As a caregiver, you often neglect your own needs and forget about your own mental, emotional, social, and spiritual health. If you are at any of these stages right now, this book is most important for you! The decisions you make right now may determine the picture of your life in the bonus years. Barbara Atkins tells you how to get your life back and live a fulfilling life on a continuous upward journey.

If you are currently in your seventies, you may already be living the principles outlined in the book. In that case, this book will resonate with you and will reinforce your commitment to living a life of purpose and significance.

Whatever your age in years, now is the time for taking a deep inventory of your life. With *70 is the New 40*, you'll sort through all of your experiences and resources and learn new ways of using them wisely and strategically as you journey forward to significance. Ask yourself, are you really fulfilled? Are you living your dreams or are you just caught up in the day-to-day routines of life—letting circumstances control and drive you, rather than you driving your life. A long time ago, I learned from my wise mother, "some people make things happen, some people watch things happen, and some people wonder what happened." Which group of people are you in?

If you're ready to make things happen, but don't know where to begin with the many daily tasks and decisions on your plate, Barbara is the mentor you need to help you become unstressed and unstoppable. As a Life Transition Coach with over thirty-five years of CEO experience, she helps you navigate this road called life with her tips for living. Use this book as your guide to write your own course.

In Chapter One, Barbara shares with us her story of transformation at forty, the impact it had on her life as she moved forward, and how those lessons learned provided fuel to do extraordinary things at seventy. In Chapter Two, we learn to examine our ideas about aging, how to change, and how to get our negative perceptions about aging in check. In Chapter Three, Barbara shows us how to get our innate power back and use this power to propel us forward when the doldrums of life get us down, and how to get unstuck. Chapter Four, my favorite chapter, opens us up to a new vision of life unfolding. "The New 70/40 Curve of Life" is a backdrop model to map our personal plans for new beginnings. We can choose the stereotypical bell-shaped curve and let circumstances drive us downward, or we can choose to reach for higher power and continue to ride the rollercoaster of life upward.

In Chapter Five, she shows us how healthy living is most important in living your best life. From taking control of chronic disease, to practicing holistic living, to controlling your environment, Barbara takes real information that those in public health have known for years and makes it transparent and easy to follow. She brings it to you in the real world and gives you a "can do" plan for living healthier through the power of holistic living and the mystical powers of unconditional giving.

In Chapter Six, she shows us how to transform our past and current successes, talents, and passions into significance in the bonus years, and how to leave a legacy for others to build upon. In this chapter, it all comes together in developing your life plan.

Finally, in Chapter Seven, Barbara leaves us with seventy guided principles for living the bonus years now, helping us to become our passionate, loving, authentic selves.

Why does this book work?

- It includes principles of success that work and are sustainable.
- It is the glue for pulling it all together—mind, body, spirit, finances, and relationships.
- It is positive in every sense of the word.
- It will empower individuals, organizations, and communities.
- It helps you find the partners and resources to implement your plan.
- It's a system for living a life of significance at any age.

This inspiring autobiographical philosophy on living life to the utmost is both engaging and uplifting. Barbara has written the vision and made it plain. All you have to do is read it and take action.

I am excited that the world is about to see another perspective on the images of aging and the value this perception has in inner and outer beauty. I challenge you to read this book, implement its principles, and let it bring about dramatic changes in your view of aging gracefully throughout life.

Dr. Damita J. Zweiback

Acknowledgments

Thanks and appreciation to my protégé and friend Damita Zweiback for her incredible support and encouragement to write this book. I also thank her for reading and editing multiple drafts.

My appreciation and thanks to Andrea and Johnny Harrison, the Rev. Charles Adams and the Rev. Reginald Steele for their spiritual guidance and reminder that "I can do all things through Christ who strengthens me." *(Philippians 4:13, NIV)*.

I thank my mastermind partners Eve Black and Judy Smith for sharing their expertise and insights. Thanks also to my mentor and friend Earl Proctor who continuously supports me in my endeavors. To Jason Cowans, Kim Toth, Bonnie Mattick, Lisa Pozzoni and Joanne Hunold: thanks for your wisdom and resources. I owe you my sincere gratitude.

Special thanks to my coach, Raquel R. Robinson, an angel in disguise, for her kindness, patience, and perseverance in helping me take the quantum leap. Her awesome coaching techniques guided me through painful phases of transition to a road of new beginnings.

And finally, I give my gratitude to my daughter-in-law, Leslie Nichols, for her unwavering belief in me that I could turn my dreams deferred into dreams realized.

Chapter 1

Introduction

"The Master said, 'At fifteen I set my heart on learning; at thirty I took my stand; at forty I came to be free from doubts; at fifty I understood the Decree of Heaven; at sixty my ear was attuned; at seventy I followed my heart's desire without overstepping the line."
~Confucius (551-479 B.C.)

Free from Doubts

When I turned forty, my life changed. It didn't necessarily go from better to worse or from worse to better, but something was different. I couldn't describe it to friends, was barely even aware of it, and didn't know how to respond to it. The more I tried to dismiss the feelings and just carry out my daily routines or doing what others expected of me—work, family, home, making time for relationships, and so forth—the more nothing seemed to fit. The change that took place was not due to any particular external circumstances or grand events, but resulted from small, subtle sparks of enlightenment that occurred daily. I can best describe it as an internal cleansing of fears, doubts, and second-guesses

1

about who I was and how I wanted to live my life. My soul became radiant. My internal belief system became filled with passion, hope, dreams, and joy, unlike at any other time before.

At forty, I became more focused on being happy, taking notice of beautiful people, objects, and moments that filled my heart with joy and freedom. I sorted through all the things that engaged my energy and began peeling away the layers of stuff that seemed to zap my spirit and cause stress. I took deliberate steps to surround myself with nature and with people who had a divine connection in my life. As I embraced this higher level of consciousness and self-assuredness my life took on a new meaning of principle and direction. At forty, I was mentally and emotionally free to be a woman of confidence. Perhaps Andy Rooney, CBS Correspondence, described it best . . .

A woman over forty will never wake you in the middle of the night and ask, "What are you thinking?" She doesn't care what you think. If a woman over forty doesn't want to watch the game, she doesn't sit around whining about it. She does something she wants to do, and it's usually more interesting. Women over forty are dignified. They seldom have a screaming match with you at the opera or in the middle of an expensive restaurant. Of course, if you deserve it, they won't hesitate to shoot you if they think they can get away with it. Older women are generous with praise; they know what it's like to be unappreciated . . . Older women are forthright and honest. They'll tell you right off if you are a jerk, if you are acting like one. You don't ever have to wonder where you stand with her."

Now, in my seventies, this phenomenon is occurring again, even more profoundly and significantly than it did thirty years ago. Words cannot describe this pinnacle plateau experience. My mind is focused with vigor and vitality as I pursue my bonus years with renewed purpose and meaning. My days are exhilarating, warm, loving, spiritual, passionate, and glorious. I feel like a mature rose in full bloom, whose roots have been nurtured, cultivated, pruned, and loved. Its beauty can be seen from its inner core to its outer petals, retaining consistent true colors, strength, and fragrance-producing radiance. In this miraculous second period of discovery and infinite choices, I'm taking quantum leaps without limitations.

For many, this awakening happens in the fifth and eighth decades. A light comes on, and a new sense of maturity, awareness, and self-discovery emerges and establishes itself in every physical, emotional, and mental aspect of life. The validity of the way you measure your life is no longer based on external circumstances, but on your own assurance of independence and direction. Your attitude changes as you find circumstances and people that once stressed you don't bother you anymore. Your life is focused on the pursuit of new dreams, new realities and a new *you*.

But it's not easy. This process of self-rediscovery can sometimes bring about significant changes and can be quite painful, emotionally. Relationships, jobs, living arrangements, and belief systems may change, as fears fall by the wayside and you plug into a higher consciousness. If you let the pain of change cloud your thinking, you may miss the 'aha' moment. It wasn't until I began to pray and ask the Creator to reveal what was happening in my life that I became aware that this was an opportunity for a blessing. As more was revealed to me, I learned that I wasn't going crazy, and God wasn't punishing me for all the past wrongs I had committed; I came to realize that this transformation was a time to explore, create, examine, and take action.

When you embrace what God has in store for you, you feel physically and mentally grateful, and your life becomes radiant. This internal grace shines through, and your physical outer appearance glows with a different complexion. This beauty is more than skin deep and is far more radiant than in any prior decade. With radiance comes a youthful, almost playful energy. People, events, and circumstances that add value to your life naturally flow to you. It is "The Secret" that those who have experienced it write about.

Follow Your Heart's Desires

As I began to describe the phenomenal period of significance after age seventy, I realized that the need to follow one's heart's desires at this stage of life is not new. Throughout history, people all over the world have decided to embrace this quantum shift. For example, Juanita Jewel Craft was elected to a seat on the Dallas City Council at age seventy-three; John Paul Stevens, who turned eighty-nine in April 2009, is the oldest sitting Supreme Court justice; at seventy-seven, John Glenn became the oldest astronaut to fly in space; Benjamin Franklin helped draft the Declaration of Independence at age seventy; at seventy-five, Warren Buffett gave a $30 billion contribution to the Bill and Melinda Gates Foundation. Cancer survivor Barbara Hillary became one of the oldest people, at age seventy-five, and the first black woman, to reach the North Pole.

Many Nobel laureates have been well beyond age seventy for their life's work. For example, Doris Lessing was eighty-eight when she won the 2007 Nobel Prize in literature, and Leonid Hurwicz was ninety when he won his award in economics the same year. Harry Truman received an honorary civic law degree from Oxford University at age seventy-two; Ronald Reagan was re-elected president at age seventy-three. Also at age seventy-three, Larry King celebrated his fiftieth year in broadcasting.[1] Nelson Mandela was released from prison at the age of seventy-two, earned the Nobel Peace Prize at age seventy-three, and was elected president of South Africa at the age of seventy-six.[2]

What this means then, is that age seventy is a starting point for choosing to embrace life more enthusiastically and freely than ever before. This period adds more wisdom and impact to your portfolio of life. At seventy you have earned your credentials with 25,550 days and 613,200 hours of seasoned knowledge and wisdom—waiting to be reinvented in numerous ventures. It is awesome when you reach this stage in life to look back and think of how much your body, your mind, and your spirit have been through— and rejoice that you're still here to tell the story! Having lived through seven decades, I have a grip on my mental image of aging and I'm realizing new dreams in my bonus years.

The thirty-year span from forty to seventy is full of rich and priceless experiences, new knowledge, and skills, accumulated in preparation for the next journey of life—from success to significance. Yes, seventy is the new forty! Your tasks during these transformative years are to maintain your health and work your spiritual gifts. The choice is yours.

To be seventy years young is sometimes
far more cheerful and hopeful
than to be forty years old.

Oliver Wendell Holmes

"I am of the opinion
that my life belongs to the community,
and as long as I live,
it is my privilege to do for it whatever I can.
I want to be thoroughly used up when I die,
for the harder I work, the more I live.
Life is no 'brief candle' to me.
It is a sort of splendid torch, which
I have got hold of for a moment,
and I want to make it burn as
brightly as possible before
handing it on to future generations."

—George Bernard Shaw

Chapter 2

Lessons from the Valley

*"Find your passion; learn how to add value to it,
and commit to a lifetime of learning."*

~Ray Kurzweil

My mom passed away in January 2007. She was ninety-three. I felt the ending of a great era, and mourned the loss to the world of her contributions and gifts. Three years before, we had celebrated her ninetieth birthday with a beautiful tribute from children, grandchildren, other relatives, and hundreds of friends. As I considered the meaning of this event, I began to think about my phases of aging, and asked myself, *what's next for me? What will be said at my ninetieth birthday tribute? What mark will I want to leave on the world, and what legacy will I leave for the next generation?*

When I turned seventy, I wasn't excited about this decade of life. I didn't quite make the connection between forty and seventy until I reviewed my life's portfolio of memoirs, events, accomplishments and failures. I then recalled and studied the lives of family members past and present as much as I could. There were times of stress, pain, and challenges. However, my search into the past unveiled a rich life given to me by God, through my parents, relatives, community, friends, and mentors. I found pillars of sustainable strength in these allies who engaged in life through giving and sharing with others. I found it **was** observing my mom's humility and love for others that **has** had the greatest impact on how I view mature aging today.

Mom, a petite 4'11" African and Native American, was a pillar of strength, whose outer appearance portrayed kindness, unselfishness, and endearing love for family, friends, and animals. This reflection was illuminated by her deep spiritual beliefs and inner beauty. She looked thirty to forty years younger than her ninety-three years. Her complexion was smooth, wrinkle free, and soft to the touch. Her long black hair showed minimal signs of gray. Her young appearance was less due to genes and more to do with her positive outlook on life and understanding her purpose for living.

Aging was not an issue discussed in the family because it was understood that age is just a number. Mom was more concerned with the quality of life lived rather than with the number of years lived. Her positive image and her practice of a healthy lifestyle were strengthened by her faith, patience, high self-esteem, and confidence. These simple basic characteristics allowed her to transition through her bonus years and age gracefully. Her wisdom touched the lives of everyone she encountered, both young and old. She was passionate about her relationship with the Creator, and religiously practiced her God-given fruits of the spirit—"love, joy, peace, patience, kindness, goodness, faithfulness, gentleness, and self-control". *Galatians 5:2-23(NIV).*

Thinking about the significance of my mother's life and her vibrant youthfulness, I began to consider my own background and strengths, sense of empowerment, and youthful joy. I also thought of other women I have met through the years who are living life to the fullest in their later years. What is it that we have in common? Is there something about our past, the way we were raised, our belief systems, or something else that gives the renewing strength to live life purposefully?

Perhaps in my story you may find a little of your own. It was the sound of the train that I heard every day, for eighteen years, that echoed questions in my mind about life, humans, and our natural habitat. I was born and raised in the heart of the coalfields in southeastern West Virginia. Family, education and Christian development gave me a foundation for facing life's challenges and opportunities. I shared a modest home with my Mom, Dad, and five siblings. Our home was in a valley surrounded by huge mountains densely covered with trees that looked like bunches of broccoli in the spring and summer, a cascade of nature's colors during the fall, and a canvas of white wonderland in the winter. These images from my early childhood gave me an appreciation of nature as a gift from my Creator.

I shared many happy and sad moments in this valley. During those years of growth and development, focus was on family, values, education, and enjoying   nature. For **six** years, I was the only female child, growing up among seventeen male cousins and uncles. What a rich experience to enjoy! I was showered with love and mentored by men of valor who instilled in me a high level of confidence, self-esteem, and integrity. I learned at an early age how to be competitive, strong willed, determined, and a risk taker. Throughout elementary school and on through senior high school, I was always challenged to compete. As a result, I was a high achiever.

When I entered junior high school, my career choice was to become a mortician. My dad, who stood at a towering height of 6'7," had a different idea for his firstborn. In addition to his working in the coalmines, he owned the one and only grocery store in our community. It was his decision that I drop my science curriculum and enroll into business courses. Dad's entrepreneurial vision for the future was much broader than mine.

I agreed with his suggestions and learned quickly it was the right choice. I took a variety of business courses, including bookkeeping and typing. Typing was where I excelled.

A few months prior to my graduation, an explosion in the mines where Dad worked shocked the community. Several men were trapped beneath the earth's surface and were killed. Fortunately, my dad missed the explosion and was able to get out of harm's way. He never returned to the mines. This was the first of many turning points in my life.

Dad, along with several close friends, sought employment in the automotive industry in Detroit, and was hired by Ford Motor Company. Eventually, my mother joined him, and got a job at Ford as well. I stayed in West Virginia to care for my five siblings until the school term ended.

Upon my graduation from high school, we all emigrated to Michigan. When we arrived, via Greyhound bus, I looked up at the sky and thought I had died and gone to heaven. I'd never seen the sky that close to earth. It seemed as if you could reach up and touch the clouds. After being in the valley so long, I felt as if I was at the top of the mountain— my world had a different view from the top.

Time to Reinvent

By the end of my thirties, a miraculous life began to unfold. College, marriage, and children were transitions that provided me with some of life's greatest opportunities. I was on an apex of self-discovery, a vision of new interest and excitement was stirring in my mind.

My first entry into the world of business came at age thirty-seven as a direct sales distributor of cosmetics. Within four years my sales achievements had broken company records. This was the platform I needed to test my entrepreneurial strengths and capabilities. Following in my father's footsteps at age forty-one I began to seize new business opportunities and became an entrepreneur. Little did I know I would use the skills from a high school typing class to establish a word processing company and turn it into a multi-million dollar business. In addition, my husband and I jointly owned an executive search firm, in which we recruited professionals and college graduates for entry-level positions with Fortune 500 companies. Unfortunately, Dad passed away before he could witness the benefits of his urging and the powerful impact he'd had on my life.

My transition period during the forties gave credence and meaning to the word maturity. It was a time of change: mental, physical and spiritual growth, challenges and decisions. Later, as can be expected in life, the unexpected happened. Without warning business-related issues became paramount, and the sudden death of my husband left me unprepared to face an uncertain future. Nine months later, my only daughter died after a long battle with multiple sclerosis. The emotional tsunami of coping with these losses and my own health challenges brought me to a crossroad of options. As a result, I closed both companies and opted to retire at age sixty-four.

As I disengaged myself from traditional work, retirement meant leisure, travel, playing as much golf as I could, and focusing on my rose garden. This lasted about four years. I became dissatisfied with too much idle time. My mind was in turmoil as I sought answers to life's purpose and meaning. I felt stuck and useless, because I was not using my God-given talents, knowledge, skills, experience, and wisdom to benefit myself or others. My quest in life had always been to use my life to contribute, help others, and leave a legacy. Four years after retirement, I decided the rocking chair was not an option. I had dreams to fulfill and a mission to accomplish. I was too young to retire!

I began to search for life's meaning from the inside—trying to find answers, and trying to decide what would be next for me. I decided to write my life plan, guided by a personal vision statement of what mattered most to me, followed by goals and objectives to achieve that vision. It was time to move from the successes of the past on to significance.

I let go of non-productive and mental weight-bearing functions affecting my life, re-ordered priorities, and wrote a life plan to guide my actions, with timelines for achievement. Then, I took action.

I opted for a new lifestyle and started on a journey toward new accomplishments. The first step was to relocate to a new environment and explore new scenery. At the age of seventy-two, I downsized, packed-up, and journeyed across the country from Detroit to Arizona. The idea of implementing my plan became exciting and fun. Life has never been the same since.

I plunged into new endeavors, which gave me a feeling of revitalization, accompanied by a sense of an emerging "new self." As I settled into my new community, I began to network, and connect with new friends and activities. In the process, I encountered two types of people: (1) those who fit the traditional, stereotypical images of aging, and (2) those whose ideas and attitudes about aging were positive and unstoppable.

It's Your Time

Those who fit the traditional aging stereotypes seemed to have been beaten by life's harsh winds—economic conditions, midlife crises, and were unprepared for retirement. The others, ageless Mat-Gens (mature generation), are the new "hip" culture whose time has come. They are emerging and changing the social climate of the twenty-first century. They are not the seniors of yesterday; they are in bloom, redefining retirement, and rising like the sun over the highest mountain. They are making enduring marks and innovative footprints in the pavement for future generations. They are a revolution abounding!

As a retirement life coach, I found a need, and connected with both cohorts to offer retirement readiness programs that emphasize the value of connecting life planning to financial planning for a balanced, holistic approach to the next phase of life.

Take a moment now and consider which group you might identify with or already belong. Which group have you been plugging your thinking into? How have you been spending your time and your energy, and with whom?

Write your answers to these questions on the following pages.

Write your outlook on life as it is today?
In which group does your thinking seem to fit?

_____

_____
_____
_____
_____
_____
_____
_____
_____
_____
_____
_____
_____
_____
_____
_____
_____
_____
_____
_____
_____
_____
_____
_____
_____

_____

_____

_____

_____

_____

_____

_____

_____

_____

_____

_____

_____

_____

_____

_____

_____

_____

_____

_____

_____

_____

_____

_____

_____

_____

How have you been spending your
time and your energy, and with whom?

_____
_____
_____
_____
_____
_____
_____
_____
_____
_____
_____
_____
_____
_____
_____
_____
_____
_____
_____
_____
_____
_____
_____
_____

_____

_____

_____

_____

_____

_____

_____

_____

_____

_____

_____

_____

_____

_____

_____

_____

_____

_____

_____

_____

_____

_____

_____

_____

_____

60 SECONDS

I have only just a minute,
Only sixty seconds in it.
Forced upon me, can't refuse it.
Didn't seek it, didn't choose it.
But it's up to me
to use it.
I must suffer if I lose it.
Give account if I abuse it.
Just a tiny little minute,
but eternity is in it.

—Anonymous writer

Chapter 3

Get a Grip on Your Mental Images of Aging

When it comes to staying young,
A mind-lift beats a face-lift any day.
~Marty Bucella

It's In the Mind's Eye

Have you ever wondered what images of aging really look like? Have you thought about your image as you pass through the decades? Is your true, authentic self showing as you age? If not, how do you make it happen? I pondered these questions myself when I reached my eighth decade. As I review the portfolio of my life, I pause and consider where I have been, where I wish to go, who I wish to be, and what I wish to do now in my bonus years.

Over the years, we realize age is only a number on the biological clock—ticking to the tune of the Creator's time. We know aging does not discriminate based on gender, orientation, race, or social status. Everyone participates equally, twenty-four hours a day, seven days a week. So why do images of aging frighten so many of us? Is it because society has been conditioned to think about frail individuals, no longer able to care for or think for themselves? Is the process of aging synonymous with the disappearance of beauty and strength?

There are some individuals who reach their fifties, sixties, and beyond and literally shut down, sink into depression, and succumb to myths associated with stereotypes of aging. Myths such as: *you're too old; you can't do that; why are you returning to school?—college is for the young; no one will hire you.* These people buy into that fixed notion of RETIREMENT, which means "end" or "quit," and resort to a sedentary lifestyle on the couch or in a rocking chair.

I'M RETIRED
(This is as dressed up as I get)

These types of images have little to do with the facts of life and everything to do with how you feel, look, or engage in mental, social, and physical activities. When mental images of aging are used positively, wisely, and effectively, they can and will provide a source of new meaning, purpose, and enthusiasm to your life. At the base of these images are powerful components of your six senses: sight, hearing, smell, taste, touch, and intuitive thought.

The most powerful component is that of thought—the mind's eye. Here is where the foundation of your belief system, your core values, and your faith shape your ideas about life and whether you succumb to its challenges and slow down, or ride the highway of life with momentum and excitement into the "bonus years."

Your personal image of aging is your perception of who you are and who you wish to be. You might say your *inner image* is the spirit of your authentic self, while the *physical image* is your appearance to the outside world—simply a printout of your inner thoughts, emotions, and spirit manifested into the physical dimensions of your body's health and lifestyle. Often, this is where chains of pain and challenges show up, not as a *natural* part of aging, but as an *interruption* in the graceful biological process of aging.

We know that so many of the conditions and dis-eases that we associate with aging can often be prevented or in fact their onset delayed if we just take preventive steps earlier in your lives.

— Julie Bishop

A poor mental attitude manifested into the physical being is sometimes where chronic conditions begin to emerge and inhibit identification with a natural, positive, vibrant, and radiant aging process. The secret is that it's not natural! Aging—getting older—does not determine a person's ability, energy, or enthusiasm for following dreams and pursuing happiness. You can adjust your pictures to include the many choices and options available throughout life's transitions. Doing this successfully requires you to get a grip on these images and force them to function in a way that is beneficial to the cell tissues of your body.

If you have reached age seventy, congratulations are in order for choosing to read this book. You are not at all interested in settling and withering away. If you're not there yet, congratulations to you as well, for taking time to learn what may be in store for you! You will not be using the phrase "If I knew then what I know now…"

By this time in your life, you may already be familiar with many of the "thought" leaders, who describe the "power of positive thinking" and how "it all begins in the mind," and other such common expressions. You may be saying to yourself, *Yes, I've heard this all before, but there's more to life than that,* or *Things happen that are beyond my control,* or you may have also heard by now, some variation of, *It's not what happens to you, it's how you respond*, and more.

Keep in mind that these statements are positive affirmations that support you and help you overcome barriers. But unless they are coupled with and connected to your physical and spiritual health and the actual actions that are required for you to take charge of your life, they won't work. That's what this book is about. It shows you how to connect these components and live a fulfilling life, no matter where you are on your journey—in your 20s, 30s, 40s, 50s or already in your bonus years!

> *There is a fountain of youth; it is your mind, your talents, the creativity you bring to your life and the lives of the people you love. When you learn to tap this source, you will have truly defeated age.*
>
> *Sophia Loren*

Mind Over Matter

What is your perception of aging? I believe it's both a mystical and spiritual aspect of life. It's a dream manifested in the mind of every individual, a dream that sets the stage for purposeful and meaningful living. It begins with your mental images, with a *thought* in mind. What you conceive and believe sends signals throughout the body affecting your emotions and feelings; these emotions are revealed in your actions. Your vertical connection to your higher being (spirit) serves as the controller for the entire body system. The physical (external) is only a display or printout of what is programmed on the inside. It is not the number of years in your life that matters; it's the quality of living in those years that matters most. This universal truth is as important today as it was in earlier years. It is the **Y-O-U** that defines your image. It's **Y**our **O**pportunity to **U**nderstand your purpose on earth.

The "bonus years," then, are the years on the horizon, taking you into the next phase of living. Along these years are beams of positive images of aging, which highlight and pave the way toward a new journey. Your life's portfolio of the past provides a foundation for re-creating your vision, setting new priorities, and reinventing yourself for decades to come. *70 is the New 40* is a combination of beliefs, values, and perceptions of many holistic factors that shape our lives from day to day and give them meaning and satisfaction. It reflects the degree to which you see your own maturation process as a time of emotional and psychological vitality and vibrancy, full of potential for dynamic and ongoing growth.[3]

Take a moment now to reflect on your mental images of aging. On the next several pages, write down your own ideas and perceptions of yourself. Look into the mirror of your mind. Who do you see now? What do you want to change? Who do you wish to be? Reflect on this and on your inner personal self—today, and where you see yourself in the next decade. How wide is the gap? At the end of the page, make a commitment to yourself to do something every day toward achieving your goals. In the rest of the book, I walk you through the strategies for reaching radiant living.

Write your personal ideas and
perceptions about aging.

Barbara Penn Atkins

How do you view your physical
and mental state today?

_____

_____

_____

_____

_____

_____

_____

_____

_____

_____

_____

_____

_____

_____

_____

_____

_____

_____

_____

_____

_____

_____

_____

_____

Barbara Penn Atkins

Reflect on your personal vision for the future.
Where do you see yourself in the next decade?

_____

_____

_____

_____

_____

_____

_____

_____

_____

_____

_____

_____

_____

_____

_____

_____

_____

_____

_____

_____

_____

_____

_____

_____

_____

Barbara Penn Atkins

_____

_____

_____

_____

_____

_____

_____

_____

_____

_____

_____

_____

_____

_____

_____

_____

_____

_____

_____

_____

_____

_____

_____

Reflect on your personal vision for the future.
What doors do you feel are open to
you at this stage of life?

_____

_____

_____

_____

_____

_____

_____

_____

_____

_____

_____

_____

_____

_____

_____

_____

_____

_____

_____

_____

_____

_____

_____

_____

_____

_____

_____

_____

_____

_____

_____

_____

_____

_____

_____

_____

_____

_____

_____

_____

_____

_____

_____

_____

_____

_____

_____

My Commitment to My Goals

_____

_____

_____

_____

_____

_____

_____

_____

_____

_____

_____

_____

_____

_____

_____

_____

_____

_____

_____

_____

_____

_____

_____

_____

Barbara Penn Atkins

Chapter 4

Discover Your Power!

"Today, I want you to become aware that you already possess all the inner wisdom, strength and creativity needed to make your dreams come true. This is hard for most of us to realize because the source of this unlimited personal power is buried so deeply beneath the bills, the car pool, the deadlines, the business trip, and the dirty laundry that we have difficulty accessing it in our daily lives."

~ Sarah Ban Breathnach

Discover Your Power

All people have personal powers that help carry them through life's trials, errors, and successes. For some, the power has become dim over the years and is buried so deep in the psyche that it's no longer detectable. A belief system of powerlessness and lack of control can limit us from fully taking charge of our own life and happiness. The good news is that power is always with you and can be restored through a process of rediscovery, belief, and faith. You can even expand your personal power to a much higher level and broader dimension than ever before.

In order to discover your personal power you must first understand several shapes that life often takes.

View of a Life Portfolio

Have you ever thought of your life as being housed in a portfolio file? This is your mental storage cabinet where your memories, knowledge, experience, skills, wisdom, and personal struggles are stored. It's there for you to open at any time and extract only what you wish to remove. You can choose what will help you proceed to the next phase of life on a positive note. Take a look at your portfolio of life. It may resemble a roller-coaster full of triumphs and failures. These ups and downs are charted on a bell-shaped curve, showing the emotional and physical events that have happened to you, by you, and sometimes even for you by the Creator.

The bell-shaped curve can represent life from two points of view—tangible and intangible—and the rollercoaster can represent life's journey of ups and downs. The tangible focuses on an accumulation of material wealth required to sustain a series of life's events, including the hierarchy of needs, education, goals, career, and family. These are assigned to the left side of the curve.

Figure A

View of Life

Bell Curve of Life

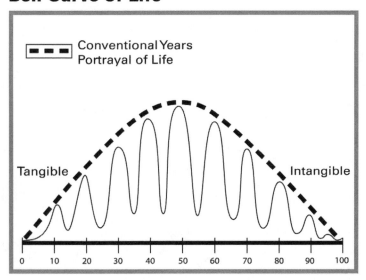

From the time you enter the workforce to the time when you are getting ready to leave, the reason for work is fourfold: to earn money for your labor, to achieve specific goals, to enhance your quality of life, and to savor the sense of fulfillment that having money can bring. Among the primary goals of saving and accumulating wealth are buying things that we think add value to life, and financing old age and retirement.

Along the tracks of the rollercoaster are markers indicating each decade, with 10, 20, 30, 40, and 50 on the left, and 60, 70, 80, and beyond on the right. Each curve on the rollercoaster symbolizes a new beginning, middle, and end of each decade, and the end of one stage is the beginning of the next. Within each curve, there are times of learning, physical and mental changes, social changes, and new discoveries that enable growth.

In decades one and two of the transitional years—birth to young adulthood—you initiate new discoveries, while passing through multiple changes in social, physiological, and psychological stages. Images of aging at this stage have little if any significance. There isn't much thought given to growing older or to the later years; you simply enter and exit these decades, enjoying birthday after birthday up through the thirties, with new visions, insights, and anticipation of what you see as your next age, always looking forward to life's new experiences.

Somewhere in the thirties or earlier, life's fundamentals get your attention, and you start to build a foundation in which tangible achievements of life, with emphasis on finances and the accumulation of material wealth are at the center of planning and goal-setting for the future.

View of the Tangibles

To live the American dream and secure life as you establish family, home, and career often requires a balance between financial planning and life planning. As a person elects to be established in civic and community activities, there is often a conditioning of the mind to believe that the purpose of life is defined by social position, career title, and material possessions.

In order for tangibles to properly work for the good, they must have a foundation built on values, integrity, and other positive characteristics found only in intangibles, which are required to sustain life's mental, physical, and emotional well being. Tangibles have a foundation with shallow roots, while intangibles are anchored deep in within the depths of one's core.

When career work ceases and the goal to continue lifestyle comforts as planned takes a different turn, the winds of adversity can quickly blow the tangibles away.

"Riches certainly make themselves wings," writes Solomon. "They fly away as an eagle toward heaven (Proverbs 23:5, KJV)." Lee Iacocca, not long after leaving the automobile business, said, "Here I am in the twilight years of my life, still wondering what it's all about. I can tell you this: fame and fortune is for the birds, and fame is as fickle as the last response from the crowd."[4]

Here again, little thought was given to planning for a life beyond when work ceases. Life's purpose and meaning stand at a crossroads where we can make the choice to fulfill our dreams deferred and pursue enduring happiness.

As a person celebrates age forty and beyond, something mystical and magical happens. How we feel life should be measured begins to take a different form. There is an awakening of the self, and our individual independence becomes profoundly important. Emphasis on the external material trappings of the tangibles of life becomes diluted. Internally, the psyche takes on a new maturity, and it only gets better and more positive with age.

This process of self-discovery sometimes can be painful; relationships, jobs, living arrangements, or belief systems may change as the fear of failure falls by the wayside. It's your vertical connection with your higher being that brings on a higher level of consciousness and self-awareness. At this stage in life, your outward appearance begins to reflect your inward transformation.

What happens in the decade of the forties depends on these stages of life. If you have not already taken the time to establish a foundation, discover your strengths, and plan for purposeful living, you may find yourself in a run-of-the-mill mindset, going through motions on automatic pilot. The conventional way of living takes on the shape of an overarching bell curve (see Figure A). The left side of the curve shows growth from birth to midlife, arching through the fifties, and then curves downward on the right side through the sixties, seventies, and beyond. An unadventurous look at the right side of fifty depicts retirement and a decline in activity, physical and cognitive health, and sometimes, emotional health.

Retirement from years of work is often an emotional period that requires a readjustment in lifestyle and reassessment of our personal self worth. Familiar questions often come to mind, such as: *Where do I go from here? Who am I without my business card?* And, *what will I do with myself and my time*? Dr. Richard P. Johnson, noted gerontologist, says, "In order to achieve a successful transition from work to a 'new retirement' lifestyle (whatever that may be for you), we must shift our view of ourselves, and redefine who we are, reframe ourselves, and undergo a career/life reorientation."[5]

If your view of aging falls within this fixed bell-shaped pattern, you may feel as though the end of your career is the end of your purpose. You may also find yourself seeking employment, but feel as though your age is a barrier to starting a new occupation. You may be facing health challenges and feel a sense of powerlessness or that you have few years left. Whatever it is, it may be just an illusion!

> *"We suffer primarily not from our vices or our weaknesses, but from our illusions. We are haunted, not by reality, but by those images we have put in their place.*
>
> *Daniel J. Boorstin*

70 is the New 40 Curve

There is another way to view the shape of life. The "70 is the New 40 Curve!" In this curve of life, if we choose to live consciously, intentionally, and wisely, the curve doesn't decline, but continues on an upward slope of growth until eternity. There are still peaks and valleys as we approach the later years in life, but the valleys never get as low and the peaks continue to get higher **(See Figure B)**.

Beyond the top of the curve, the shadow of a new perception emerges as the dawning of a new day. The imagination is startled by a mirage of questions, concerns, and new thoughts about life and what's next. This is a crossroads, a choice to settle where we are, or to view life as an opportunity to use realities from the past to create a new vision for a bright future. It says in bold colors that it's time to set new priorities and bridge the gap between successes of the past and a purposeful future.

View of the Intangibles

The intangibles though not perceptible by touch, have power to affect visible and positive change in every **aspect of your life**. Service rendered through acts of kindness is priceless to both recipient and giver offers a sense of fulfillment.

In these *intangible* years, the basic arenas of life–family, relationships, self, health and wellness, leisure and spiritual connections—emerge as all inclusive and equally important. These arenas are not measured by material possessions or monetary wealth, but by those values within us that give purpose and meaning to life and love. Here, reflections of portfolio history dictate a new call-to-action plan. Create a new vision, and set new priorities that emphasize a purpose-driven and meaningful life. Your options and choices are there for a life of joy and happiness. In these years, take time to re-invent yourself, revisit passions, reassess what matters most, and embrace those dreams deferred.

Today, over 78 million baby boomers are glaring at the right side of the curve as they dance into decades six and seven. Those who are determined to ride the high tides of bonus waves are redefining the myths of aging and creating a new, positive image. These energetic boomers are looking forward to disengaging from their predictable careers and focusing on plans to reinvent themselves in a new lifestyle that combines their knowl-edge and passions.

If you're in the pre-boomer generation, take time to examine the curve of life you're on today. If your disengagement from work occurred between ages forty-five and fifty-five, you're most likely living the "70 is the New 40" bonus years right now, filled with choices and opportunities! You've had, or are currently having, a paradigm shift, re-inventing yourself, re-careering, and re-investing your talents.

Figure B

Bell Curve of Life

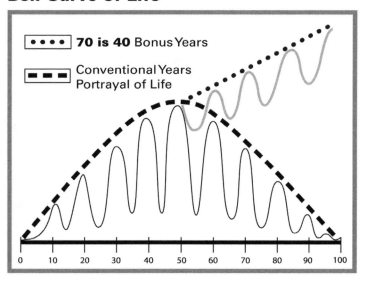

In the "70 is the New 40 Curve," the lines of life reveal life as a fabric made of fine silk threads, representing the portfolio of history and wisdom woven with the intensity of values, principles, and character. Its seam binding is a continuous learning curve, stitched with a progressive line of choices, options, and opportunities.

At seventy, the rewiring happens again, and we take on a different level of self-awareness and self-consciousness. Your image of aging and your perception of your future bonus years reside within your mind. It is up to you to give them shape and form.

At seventy, our focus is on the authentic self, where the expression of a holistic approach to living takes form. Life again has a distinct new meaning. Each period builds on a foundation of family, community, values, spirituality, and social relationships, all connected by strong pillars of education, skills, and wisdom. What has transpired during these decades chronicles our history, and has earned us the status of belonging to an elite group, known as "Mat–Gens," the Mature Generation.

Describe your major life challenges and
opportunities. Reflect and write the
personal power used in the experience

Example:	Power:
"I lost the promotion I worked so hard for."	*Learned New Skills*

Experiences continued

Write your personal power statements!

Example:

I have the power to learn from mistakes and find new talent.

_____

_____

_____

_____

_____

_____

_____

_____

_____

_____

_____

_____

_____

_____

_____

_____

_____

_____

_____

_____

_____

_____

_____

_____

_____

_____

_____

_____

_____

_____

_____

_____

_____

_____

_____

_____

_____

_____

_____

_____

_____

_____

_____

_____

_____

_____

_____

_____

Personal power statements continued

_____

_____

_____

_____

_____

_____

_____

_____

_____

_____

_____

_____

_____

_____

_____

_____

_____

_____

_____

_____

_____

_____

_____

_____

Chapter 5

Take Control of Your Health and Wellness

"True enjoyment comes from activity of the mind and exercise of the body; the two are ever united."
~*Humboldt*

Take Control of the Three D's

Contrary to popular belief, poor health is not a natural consequence of getting older.[6] Although studies show that many older adults suffer from at least one or two chronic health conditions[7], such as high blood pressure, high cholesterol, arthritis, diabetes, and so forth, the good news is that many chronic health problems are preventable and can be well-managed by simple changes in lifestyle and daily habits. It's never too late to take control of your health. Prevention, quality medical treatment, and self-management of health can make a dramatic difference in your quality of life, even after the onset of a chronic condition.

Healthy lifestyle choices are the keys to a good quality of life, mental and physical well being, and a long, productive, and independent life. In this chapter, I challenge you to take control of the three Ds (**D**isease, **D**isability, and **D**epression).

Taking Control of Chronic Disease

The number one cause of death among older Americans is heart disease, followed by cancer. However, medical care has improved dramatically in last twenty years. Studies show that most diseases, including heart disease and cancer, may be prevented through simple changes in diet and exercise reduction, or if caught early enough, may be successfully treated and controlled.[8,9,10] A diagnosis of cancer is not always fatal. But, despite these advances, only about forty percent of individuals on average get proper medical exams or make lifestyle changes to improve their health.[11]

Getting routine checkups, keeping your cholesterol at a normal level, and controlling your blood pressure are among the habits you should cultivate. The greatest influences on health are weight management, exercise, nutrition, and a healthy attitude. Maintaining a healthy and fit lifestyle will decrease your risks of developing a chronic disease and will minimize your healthcare costs. A healthy and fit lifestyle includes a well-balanced diet with a serving of fresh fruits and vegetables with every meal, an active lifestyle with moderate body movement at least three times per week for thirty minutes each, quitting smoking or avoiding cigarette smoke and other drugs, keeping alcohol in moderation, and maintaining healthy relationships.

Disability Does Not Mean Dysfunction

About 50 million American adults have disabilities, including hearing loss, mental disability (such as dementia), physical limitation, or vision loss.[12] According to the Centers for Disease Control and Prevention, people with disabilities generally report poorer health, smoke more, are more often obese, and get less exercise than people without disabilities.[13] However, with the proper supports, people with disabilities can and do maintain active lifestyles.[14]

Depression: by Any Means, Protect Your Mind

The American Association of Geriatric Psychiatry reports an estimated twenty percent of the national population of adult's age fifty-five and over have experienced some type of mental health concern, including major depressive disorder.[15] Retirement, changes in financial status, health, social network, marital status, living arrangements, emotional abuse, or loss of mobility and independence can all trigger or contribute to depression. Depression can also be linked with physical illness and loss of function.

Depression is often unnoticed, misdiagnosed, and untreated.[16] Most people don't even realize they've fallen into a state of depression until their condition results in severe behavior change and is noticed by someone close to them. This is especially problematic if you live alone, because the likelihood of detection is reduced. Symptoms of depression include loneliness, seclusion, anger, loss of hope, unexplained moodiness, fatigue, insomnia, and loss of interest in hobbies or activities.

If you're having any of these symptoms, you may not have recognized what is happening to you, but you do not have to suffer. Depression can be treated, with or without medication. The Center for Disease Control recommends several treatment options that have proven the most effective in treating older adults. Check the resource listing at the end of this book for details.

If you suspect you are depressed, consult your physician and tell him or her about your symptoms. Physicians often will not pick up on these symptoms, or may not ask, because they are focused on your physical health. You must be open to sharing your emotional state with your doctor. You may also contact the employee wellness program where you work or volunteer, if such a program exists. Other resources include neighborhood health and wellness organizations. Check your local area listings for specific contacts or the web references in the back of this book.

Other actions you can take to maintain your brain health include preventing or controlling high blood pressure, cholesterol, and diabetes, maintaining a healthy weight, quitting smoking, and maintaining a physically active lifestyle.[17] Joining a group exercise program can have dual benefits of physical activity and social support and networking. More recent studies show that meditation also shows promise in maintaining brain health.[18,19]

Practice Holistic Living

General medical practice is concerned with the body's health at the cellular, muscular, and organic levels. Holistic health is concerned with your best possible health at all levels of functioning, and includes balancing of the body's physical/genetic characteristics, environmental conditions, emotional and spiritual health, and overall quality of life. The American Holistic Medical Association supports ten principles of holistic medicine. These can be summarized into four overarching principles for holistic living: 1) Understanding your body's unique structure, 2) Environment, 3) Lifestyle, and 4) Spiritual-mind-body connection.

☐ Your unique structure: The unique individuality of your genes and cell structure describes who you are in the most physical scientific sense. Holistic health includes understanding the connection between your physical genetic makeup and the energy systems of the body. Managing this connection is essential to preventing illness, curing the body, relieving symptoms, and eliminating factors that contribute to poor health.

☐ Your environment: The communities in which you live, work, and play are as important to your health and wellness as what you do and what you eat. For years now, the connection between environmental pollutants and their effects on health has been in the public eye. While there is still much work to be done to promote clean air, health officials are also recognizing the effects of clean and safe neighborhoods on health. Walkable communities with less traffic, easy access to parks, groceries, schools, health facilities, and civic engagements are contributing factors to physical, mental, and emotional health.[20,21] Hazardous and stressful environments have also been shown to impact mental and physical well-being. Dilapidated and depressed neighborhoods contribute to a sense of hopelessness and stress in the body, thereby increasing likelihood of developing a chronic illness.[22] Your internal environment has an impact on your health as well. Disorganization, clutter, unfinished projects, broken or non-working household items can also be stressful to you health.

☐ Your lifestyle: Making healthy practices a normal part of your everyday routine can have dramatic impact on your health and well-being. Introducing small incremental changes over time will be more likely to stick than big, radical changes all at once. Simple changes in diet, such as eliminating sugar, salt, or fattening creams can have great benefits. Eating meals earlier in the day will help burn more calories as you continue to be active, as opposed to eating in the late evening when our bodies tend to slow down. Reducing caloric intake and burning calories through exercise and movement will help keep your weight healthy and manageable. Simple exercises, such as walking, weight lifting, and stretching for flexibility, is recommended as starting points, once you've consulted your physician. Listed in the further reading section are various websites for additional information on diet and exercise programs for older adults. Other healthy lifestyle practices include regular check-ups and medical exams, not smoking or abusing drugs, moderate or no alcohol, safe sex practices, and stress management through leisure activities, adequate rest, massage therapy, and medication and relaxation.

☐ Your spiritual and mental connection: This is the programmatic level of holistic living: how you think and what you feel is determined by the messages you choose to program into your mind. You have an innate mental and emotional healing system within you, which begins with unconditional love of self and others. When you tap into this power, you attract into your life all that is in divine harmony with you. There are various ways to harness this powerful system and make it work for you as the Creator intended: daily prayer and meditation, yoga, aromatherapy, massage therapy, and energetic forms of movement combined with conscious thought are all beneficial to keeping the mind and body in balance. The very act of taking control of your health through continuous learning and individual-centered empowerment can influence your health status. This has been proven in chronic disease self-management courses that incorporate various forms of light exercise, and health management techniques, including group learning and support."[23]

The Priceless Value of Giving

One area of health that is often overlooked is the art of charitable giving. When most people think of charitable contributions, they think of the psychological rewards of giving money, time, donations, volunteer activities, and other gifts. The art of giving has a physical impact on your well-being as well. When you give, it is unconditional, and provides a comforting feeling. Comforting feelings are generated by the release of endorphins in the body, which also decreases pain and stress and enhances the immune response system, thereby signaling calmness and healing.[24]

Spiritual health is the fulcrum or crowbar that links and balances your mental, physical, and emotional being. Sharing your time, gifts, and talents with others, and

> *We make a living by what we get, We make a life by what we give.*
>
> Winston Churchill

cultivating relationships with family, friends, and other social networks is just as important in your bonus years, if not more, as any other time of life. These are only a few factors that you need in your quest for health and wellness on your journey through the bonus years.

Through the art of giving and a balanced holistic lifestyle, you transform the three Ds of disease, disability, and depression to:

➤ Discovery—an infinite vertical connection that lifts the level of your consciousness to a state of revelation and awareness.

➤ Discipline—a higher power of understanding, self-control, and internal enlightenment.

➤ Dedication—a spiritual deepening of convictions and a broadened base of confidence and commitment.

Right now, take an assessment of your lifestyle. Are there areas in which you can make small changes that would have a dramatic impact on your health? Use the worksheets on the next page to assess your physical and emotional health. Note symptoms you've been experiencing, and questions you might consider talking with a health professional about. Assess your home and work environments. Are they healthy and hazard-free? Is there harmony? Is there something you can do at work to make it more pleasant, such as cleaning and organizing your desktop, bringing in a plant or fresh flowers, hanging pictures of family, or displaying, items that put you in good spirits?

> *"To insure good health: eat lightly, breathe deeply, live moderately, cultivate cheerfulness, and maintain an interest in life."*
>
> —*William Londen*

My personal lifestyle inventory

My physical health status:

_____

_____

_____

_____

_____

_____

_____

_____

_____

_____

_____

_____

_____

_____

_____

_____

_____

_____

_____

_____

_____

_____

_____

My environment at home and at work:

My current healthy daily habits (to keep doing):

_____

_____

_____

_____

_____

_____

_____

_____

_____

_____

_____

_____

_____

_____

_____

_____

_____

_____

_____

_____

_____

_____

_____

Poor health habits I need to change:

My spiritual growth:

_____

_____

_____

_____

_____

_____

_____

_____

_____

_____

_____

_____

_____

_____

_____

_____

_____

_____

_____

_____

_____

_____

_____

_____

_____

_____

_____

My charitable contributions:
_____

_____

_____

_____

_____

_____

_____

_____

_____

_____

_____

_____

_____

_____

_____

_____

_____

_____

_____

_____

_____

_____

_____

_____

_____

My daily plan for eating healthy and burning calories.

Monday: _____

_____

_____

_____

_____

_____

_____

_____

Tuesday: _____

_____

_____

_____

_____

_____

_____

_____

Wednesday: _____

_____

_____

_____

_____

_____

Thursday:

_____

_____

_____

_____

_____

_____

_____

Friday:

_____

_____

_____

_____

_____

_____

_____

Saturday:

_____

_____

_____

_____

_____

_____

_____

_____

Chapter 6

Transition from Success to Significance

"The key to realizing a dream is not to focus on success, but significance—and then even the small steps and little victories along your path will take on even greater meaning."

~*Oprah Winfrey*

Many of us, in our years of work and service to careers, have experienced success, or successful outcomes. Success is defined differently by different people, but the common thread is that it is the outcome of some effort. Some examples of successful results include getting projects done on time and within a budget; successfully meeting clients' needs over and over again; success in growing a business, a department, or a program, for example. If you are actively planning your retirement, no matter what your age, you may be asking, *why should I transition if I'm already a success?* Or *what's the difference?*

Because successful job outcomes and similar types of results are intellectually and psychologically gratifying, retirement from years of work is often an emotional period. Therefore, it requires a readjustment of lifestyle and reassessment of your personal self-worth that isn't necessarily defined by your business card. In your quest for a life of purpose and fulfillment, infinite opportunities and options exists for you to pursue. Whether it is choosing another career or becoming an entrepreneur, a commitment to give of your time and talents is the first step to a life of personal significance. It is a reciprocal act where both yours and the receiver's needs are met in a holistic manner.

Success, then, is about results. Significance is about meaning and impact. Significance is the message that leaves a lasting change for the better in the lives of people, in the environment, or in objects encountered. The next phase of life is a time to reinvent yourself, revisit your passions, embrace those dreams deferred, and reassess what matters most to you.

Plan for Significance

It's never too early to start planning and never too late to take action for a life after work and for considering how you will transition from success to significance. Writing a life plan and connecting it to your financial plan is the beginning of this life-changing transfer. Be your own master planner and start with a vision board.

Create a collage of your ideal life as you wish it to be. Clip and arrange images to represent what life should look like. Use your imagination to empower and motivate you to action. It's important to have a clear vision of what you want your life to be. Be specific in articulating your ideas.

Next, what are your passions? What are your values? What is your purpose? Answers to these questions give you the foundation upon which to build. Be specific with the details of your thoughts; then create an image of what life will be like, based on your core values and your portfolio of experience, knowledge, and skills. Place your images on the board with descriptive statements and a projected date of completion for each function. See yourself *being* and *doing* your ideal dream. Your plan should contain four primary components: 1) your goals, dreams, and passions; 2) your current talents, skills, and experiences; 3) significant actions and activities you want to devote time and energy to; and 4) your financial and professional resources to support the achievement of your plan.

Life Goals, Dreams, and Passions

The first step in developing your plan is to know what you want. While this seems so simple, most people can't answer it in a clear concise statement that provides enough specifics to create a visual. Often, the reply is broad vague ideas of happiness and money, or a one-time adventure experience, such as to climb Mt. Everest.

Write goals that are specific, measurable, and realistic. Being realistic does not mean putting a limit to your dream; instead, it means thinking in smaller time-frames of what's possible to accomplish in one month, six months, one year, and so forth. Assign a time by which you want to achieve each of your goals. Don't be afraid to change and rewrite goals to fit your circumstances. Reinventing your life calls for an act of imagination. Think outside the traditional box for ways to redirect your life throughout the aging years. The images you portray should bring only satisfaction to you. The life plan is where making a difference in the lives of others should be placed high on your list of priorities. With the global capabilities of the Internet, expand your dreams beyond the horizons of your local community. Your ideas may lead you to places all around the world.

Current Talents, Skills, and Experience

Look at your talents, skills, and experience. What do you do well and naturally? What activities do you participate in that don't require motivation—activities that give you a natural euphoria? Think of activities that you would continue to do, regardless of the costs. What subjects have you gained an expertise in, based on the experiences you have gained over the years? How can you share these with others to create and serve meaningfully in your community? For example, if you've built model trains as a hobby for years and have taught elementary or high school, can you combine your teaching skills and model building to teach underdeveloped societies something that would improve lives?

If you've been a stay-at-home mom, do you have a great system for running an organized household that young mothers or others could benefit from? More and more examples of these combinations can be found all around you. The Civic Ventures organization in San Francisco, California, for example, has an Encore Careers campaign that "focuses on creating pathways to encore careers that provide continued income doing work that is personally fulfilling and helps address some of society's biggest challenges."[25] In other words, can you expand on or repurpose your life's experiences and talents toward dream fulfillment? Think of words that resonate with you to replace the word *retirement.* Answers to these questions give you the foundation upon which to build your significance plan.

Significant Actions and Activities

In this section of your plan, write the legacy you want to leave behind. In other words, how do you want to make a difference, and to what group of people–to children, teenagers, older adults? Today's new retirees between the ages of fifty and seventy-five are career re-cyclers. Many of these new careers evolve from dreams deferred from childhood, surfacing to make a difference in the lives of others. A seventy-two-year-old pharmacist re-careers and becomes a watch repair technician for her love of watches; an executive recruiter in his seventies becomes a mid-life coach; an engineer in her sixties becomes a math teacher, or a retired military officer volunteers to build and repair furniture for a homeless shelter.

Your bonus years offer a significant opportunity to find true meaning in life. These are years for you to realize your purpose, to take action, and to make a profound statement of who you are. Now is the time to expand on your life's work from your portfolio of success to the significance of expression and meaning by offering to serve others and make this world a better place. If you haven't started—it's never too late. You need to be determined, dedicated, disciplined, and committed—to a purpose, to others, and to action.

Do you need a few tips on how, when, and where you should start? Let's start within your family, church, and community. Or, think globally. There are places in the world where millions of men, women, and children are waiting for your helping hand. Any of these are excellent places to start. If not there, look at our environment. What can you do to help protect it? Perhaps you may want to help bridge the inter-generational gap and mentor youth, sharing your wisdom and experience. Use your gifts of love to brighten a life in a local hospital, or deliver meals to the sick. Volunteer through United Way agencies or community based programs. Visit hospitals and nursing homes, pray with someone, or simply care for a homeless animal. You decide! Use your God-given talents and creative imagination as you plan the highlights of your journey for a life of significance.

Financial Resources and Professional Assistance

Preparing your life journey requires reviewing your personal essentials and making sure all other areas of your life are stable and in balance. An examination of your finances is very important at this stage. You may be transitioning from full-time employment to owning your own business, doing part-time or volunteer work, working from home, or working while on the road traveling.

Whatever your circumstances, you will need to make sure you are earning enough to support your living expenses, your leisure and social activities, and leaving enough savings for emergencies. Invest wisely, so your money works for you, instead of you working for it. If your goal is to support a charitable organization through monetary donations, plan carefully, and set aside enough funds to meet your personal goals for the cause.

As you envision your future ideal life, consider engaging professionals to help you make it a reality. Commit to a fiscal check-up periodically. Financial advisors offer guidance regarding savings and money management. Spending time with a professional retirement life coach can bridge the gap between the financial plan and life plan by addressing specific factors relevant to pre-retirement readiness and preparations for life after work ceases (see www.pennagroup.com for details).[26]

Share your vision for your lifestyle with your professional team–they will help you fit the pieces together. Understanding your goals, talents, and resources is the key to successful retirement planning.

Getting Started

To prepare for your success to significance transition, review the sample form at the end of this chapter to help you organize your next steps. Then create your plan, using the sample as a model. Be specific as to the extent of your involvement.

Next, create a visual image of what life will be like, based on your core values and your portfolio of experience, knowledge, and skills. Place your plan, along with picture images, on a board with descriptive statements, and a date to begin and complete each step in your plan of action. The value in this exercise is that you see yourself being and living your dream. This is your plan. Be flexible and willing to make adjustments to fit your changing lifestyle. For a free blank PDF copy of the life plan form, visit my website at www.sunrisebeginnings.com.[27]

My Life Plan for Significance

My Goals, Dreams, Passions	My Talents, Skills, Experience	My Opportunities for Significant Action	Actions Steps to Achieve Financial and Professional Goals (from my Advisors)
To produce documentary films about money.	Good photographer (hobby)	Have a friend in film production at the university.	Need to plan about 150 hours; Will need to stop other projects to free up time.
	Good videographer (hobby)	Will talk to my broker about ideas.	Need to purchase or rent better equipment.
	Have videographed over 15 weddings, meetings, and parties.	Can interview people about their experiences	Estimated cost (including my expenses) $25,000.
	Have taken courses in film production.	Can share film with colleges to show in their classrooms.	Find sponsors for the project before getting started.
	Like stories on the human experiences of the stock market.	Can use film to teach about human emotions when investing.	
Date to Achieve Part-Time status	**Skills to Improve, Learn About or Develop More**	**Other Relationships to Establish**	**Additional Financial and Professional Needs**
Start: September 1, 2009 Complete: June 1, 2010	Digital photography and web-based videos,	International organizations	Save $5,000 for traveling abroad.
Start: September 1, 2009 Complete: December	Enroll in a class at the university.		$349 for course.

Chapter 7

Empowered at 40 and Quantum Leaps at 70

"This is the highest wisdom that I own; freedom and life are earned by those alone who conquer them each day anew."

~Johann Wolfgang von Goethe

The paradigm shifts in my forties were a prelude to thirty years of enriched and empowered experiences. The options and choices available to me on the rollercoaster ride of life were fascinating, to say the least. It was in my forties that the stage was set for some of my highest accomplishments and achievements yet to come. During this decade, I wrote my first business plan to co-partner and start an executive search firm, which expanded into one of the largest minority-owned search firms in the country. I also boldly wrote my second business plan and launched a data entry business at the height of the recession in the mid-eighties. I started with one employee and rapidly grew the business to a staff of 185 people in less than five years, generating over $2.5

million dollars in sales. If that wasn't enough, at a Mackinac Island Conference, I challenged members of the Michigan Legislature on minimum wage legislation, served on numerous boards, and participated in various civic organizations, all while raising a family and managing a household.

Now, in my seventies, I compare my life to that of a caterpillar. Once a caterpillar has emerged from its chrysalis, there is no going back, but there is a continuous unfolding into something new, something beautiful, and something free. Like the butterfly, life at seventy, with wings fully spread, can be an outward reflection of an inner transformation. There is a heightened sense of freedom and blessings during this period of life. This isn't a multiple-choice exam where you select one among the array of choices and hope it is the correct answer; all of the choices are correct, and they are all yours. Your first task is expressing your freedom to choose to put your life into something you are passionate about. Your second task is to choose to be healthy, energetic, and full of vibrant vitality, fulfilling your purpose. You will make many other choices to rejuvenate, transform, and reinvent yourself for the next phase in your life's journey.

Quantum leaps at seventy, however, do not just happen without a map for action and a plan for implementation. Your portfolio of knowledge, experience, and wisdom is not to be buried in the tombs of the ancients, but transformed into beams of significance. Aging gracefully requires due diligence, work, patience, commitment, and perseverance, along with a holistic philosophy, and an enduring spirit. With the mind, body, and spirit in harmony with the Creator's plan, an additional thirty years of new experiences, knowledge, and wisdom are full of fresh air, freedom, and benevolence.

Priorities for the Ageless Journey

Listed below are seventy tips to help you make your bonus years an ageless journey:

1. Write a plan for your next stage of life—starting today.
2. Develop a vision for your life and create a vision board.
3. Develop a vision map—a step-by-step guide to implementing your vision.
4. Identify your ideas and perceptions about aging.
5. Define your perception of life satisfaction.
6. Cultivate and maintain a positive attitude.
7. Establish and maintain a vertical connection to your higher being.

8. Eliminate negative thoughts and distractions from your life.

9. Always do your best, look your best, and be your best.

10. Have a sense of humor—laughter is good for the soul.

11. Reassess and reorder priorities periodically.

12. Nurture healthy relationships and discontinue unhealthy ones.

13. Be active and involved in church, synagogue or religious community service, and civic activities.

14. Establish trust and maintain your integrity.

15. Stay spiritually active—find perfect rhythm in life through daily meditation and prayer.

16. Stay physically active; exercise daily.

17. Maintain a healthy mind; practice healthy habits; continuously learn new things, and expand your knowledge.

18. Create positive affirmations.

19. Eat a balanced diet, including whole foods— fruits, vegetables, and grains.

20. Know your values and personal belief system.

21. Stay socially active; stay connected to people you enjoy.

22. Leisure: Play and have fun. Take mini vacations for relaxation.

23. Travel; explore new territories; change your scenery.
24. Experience different cultures and lifestyles; meet new people.
25. Get plenty of sleep; rest and restore physical and mental strength.
26. Learn a new language, and study the customs and governments of other cultures.
27. Provide leadership and guidance to youth.
28. Share your knowledge, wisdom, and experience.
29. Mentor, coach, and tutor others.
30. Develop a financial vision; plan and map to achieve it.
31. Help others develop their own value and belief systems.
32. Sponsor and support youth organizations.
33. Chaperone students at school events.
34. Break through personal barriers.
35. Establish accountability systems; hold yourself and others to them.
36. Learn computer technology.
37. Use the Internet to connect with the world.
38. Develop global relationships.
39. Join social media networks, such as Facebook Twitter or LinkedIn.
40. Organize and simplify your life; clean out clutter.

41. Give heirlooms to family.
42. Give unused items to charity.
43. Re-purpose your talents, skills, and experiences.
44. Re-Career - start a new business.
45. Turn your hobby into an opportunity.
46. Become a consultant.
47. Journal; write your memoir; share your story.
48. Improve your communication skills.
49. Plan your legacy. How do you want to be re-membered?
50. Be a philanthropist.
51. Give unconditionally.
52. Cultivate a spirit of love for all you meet.
53. Contribute to make a difference.
54. Buy a life insurance policy and assign your favorite charity as beneficiary.
55. Leave a legacy for the next generation—a foundation for others to build upon.
56. Seek happiness in the present.
57. Appreciate nature and the natural order of the universe.
58. Begin each day with gratitude and thanksgiving.
59. Advocate: Use your voice to champion change in the political, social, and economic landscape of our country and the world.
60. Be diligent about implementing your plan.

61. Practice and improve self-discipline.

62. Set priorities and eliminate distractions.

63. Learn how to convert criticism into confidence.

64. Practice and improve time management.

65. Discover your passions and find time to engage in them often.

66. Forgive, and develop compassion.

67. Focus.

68. Take action every day.

69. Discover your strengths and find partners who balance your weaknesses.

70. Always be ready for opportunity as life unfolds.

Life is not measured in months. It is measured in moves and action. Implementing and using these principles can shift your life dramatically and quickly. Get started now. Choose seven items from the list to implement in the next thirty days. Add these to your life plan and map out the detailed steps for accomplishment. Begin with those that are the easiest for you to start doing. If you're already doing most of these, expand your vision. Create your own bucket list and make it happen.

Can you improve what you're doing? Making a change in life or lifestyle at any age can be difficult, but when your heart and mind are in harmony with your actions and the wisdom of the Creator is your guide - your soul will sing Significance!

You Are Here for a Reason!

"In this particular time and place in your life—and perhaps in the very specific challenges facing you right now—are truly the invitations to expand your capacity to be patient, courageous, flexible, and forgiving, to make wise choices, to see things from a wider perspective, and by embracing and growing through them, to become ever more fully the compassionate, insightful, aware, wise, deep, and beautiful soul that you are truly."

Caroline Joy Adams

Celebrate the New You

Select seven items from the list to start doing in the next thirty days. Write detailed steps to do each day to achieve each goal

_____

_____

_____

_____

_____

_____

_____

_____

_____

_____

_____

_____

_____

_____

_____

_____

_____

_____

_____

_____

_____

Celebrate the New You

List 50 ways to celebrate each new goal you accomplish.

_____

_____

_____

_____

_____

_____

_____

_____

_____

_____

_____

_____

_____

_____

_____

_____

_____

_____

_____

_____

_____

_____

About the Author

Barbara Penn Atkins, author, speaker, transition life coach and facilitator inspires others to plan a life of meaning and purpose. A native of West Virginia, her thirty-year career history includes owner and president of a multi-million dollar data processing company and co-owner of an executive search firm where she spent fifteen years coaching professionals in career and business development. She has worked as a sales and marketing manager and as an executive director for a non-profit agency.

While building her businesses, she maintained a committed role in civic, community, and political activities, receiving numerous awards on a state, local, and federal level, including the prestigious ATHENA Award and Federal SBA Award.

After a brief period in retirement she combined her entrepreneurial and business executive experience to launch The Penna Group, LLC. Her services include leadership development, retirement transition workshops and re-career coaching to pre and post retirees for life planning.

Her business career has been published in *Money Magazine*, *Essence*, *The Washington Post,* and other publications. She has traveled extensively throughout the United States, Caribbean, Africa, Asia and Europe. She's an avid golfer and resides in Arizona.

Further Reading

Anthony, Mitch. (2008). The New Retirementality: Planning Your Life and Living Your Dreams...at Any Age You Want. (3rd Ed.). Hoboken, NJ: Wiley and Sons.

Bolles, Richard N. and Nelson, John E. (2007). What Color is Your Parachute? for Retirement: Planning Now for the Life You Want. Berkeley, CA: Ten Speed Press.

Demetre, Danna. (2003). Scale Down: A Realistic Guide to Balancing Body, Soul & Spirit. Grand Rapids, MI: Baker Book House Company. (pp. 12-13).

Johnson, Richard P. (2001). The New Retirement Options: Discovering Your Dreams. St. Louis, MO: World Press.

Johnson, Richard P., (2001). What Color is Your Retirement? Life Options Guidebook to Discover, Plan and Live Your Retirement Dream. *Available only at:* www,retirementoptions.com

Kiyosakai, Robert T., and Lechter, Sharon L. (2000). Rich Dad Poor Dad: What the Rich Teach Their Kids— That the Poor and Middle Class Do Not! New York, NY: Warner Business Books.

Robinson, Raquel R. (2006). Renew, Refocus, and Recover! A Road Trip to the Life You Deserve. Longwood, FL: Xulon press.

Stone, Howard and Marika Stone. (2004). Too Young to Retire: 101 Ways to Start the Rest of Your Life. New York, NY: The Penguin Group.

Swindoll, Charles R. (2005). Great Days with the Great Lives: Daily Insight from Great Lives of the Bible. Nashville, TN: W Publishing Group.

Traylor, Jerry. (2006). Live Carefully: The Importance of Caring in a Life of Significance. Phoenix, AZ: Acacia Publishing.

Web site References

Sample Exercises
National Institute on Aging
http://www.nia.nih.gov/HealthInformation/Publicati
ons/ExerciseGuide

Easy Fitness Solutions
www.easyfitnesssolutions.com

**Your Guide to Lowering Your Blood Pressure
with DASH: DASH Eating Plan**
US Department of Health and Human Services
National Institutes of Health
National Heart, Lung, and Blood Institute
http://www.nhlbi.nih.gov/health/public/heart/hbp/da
sh/new_dash.pdf

Nutrition Information
Extraordinary Health, Garden of Life, Inc., W.
Palm Beach, Fl.
www.gardenoflife.com

About Depression and Older Adults
www.cdc.gov/Aging/pdf/mental_health_brief_2.pdf

Resource on Caregiving
National Alliance for Caregiving
http://www.caregiving.org

Intergenerational Programs
Experience Corps
Tutoring and mentoring kids
http://www.experiencecorps.org.

Generations United
http://www.gu.org

"We are made wise not by the recollection of our past, but by the responsibility for our future"

George Bernard Shaw

Notes

[1]Vickers, Earl. (2009). "*The Book of Your Life.*" Website: http://www.museumofconceptualart.com

[2]Cohen, Raymond. (2009). "*Ask Geezer.*" Website: http://jacksonville.com/user/profile/ask_geezer

[3]Johnson, Richard P. (2001). The New Retirement Options: Discovering Your Dreams. St. Louis, MO: World Press.

[4]Swindoll, Charles R. (2005). Great Days with the Great Lives: Daily Insight from Great Lives of the Bible. Nashville, TN: W Publishing Group.

[5]Johnson, Richard P. (2001). The New Retirement Options: Discovering Your Dreams. St. Louis, MO: World Press.

[6]Centers for Disease Control and Prevention. National Center for Chronic Disease Prevention and Health Promotion. (2009). Healthy Aging: Improving and Extending Quality of Life Among Older Americans. Atlanta, GA.

[7]National Council on Aging (NCOA). (2009) Healthy Aging Fact Sheet. Washington, DC.

[8]Johnson, Richard P. (2001). The New Retirement Options: Discovering Your Dreams. St. Louis, MO: World Press.

[9] American Heart Association. (2009). *"Blood Tests for Rapid Detection of Heart Attack."* Heart Disease Detection: A New Era in Diagnosis. Website: http://www.webmd.com

[10] Larsen, Pushpa, ND. (2008). "An Ounce of Prevention: New Possibilities for the Early Detection of Heart Disease." Website: www.naturalchoice.net/articles/heartdisease.htm

[11] Centers for Disease Control and Prevention. National Center for Chronic Disease Prevention and Health Promotion. (2009). Healthy Aging: Improving and Extending Quality of Life Among Older Americans. Atlanta, GA.

[12] Centers for Disease Control and Prevention. (2006). Disability and Health State Chartbook, 2006: Profiles of Health for Adults with Disabilities. Atlanta, GA.

[13] Federal Interagency Forum on Aging-Related Statistics. (2008). Older Americans 2008: *Key Indicators of Well-Being*. Washington, DC: US Government Printing Office.

[14] National Center for Physical Activity and Disability. (2008). Physical Activity Guidelines for Individuals with Disabilities. U.S. Department of Health and Human Services. Washington, DC.

[15] American Association of Geriatric Psychiatry (2008). Depression in Late Life: Not a Natural Part of Aging. Bethesda, MD.

[16] Centers for Disease Control and Prevention and the National Association of Chronic Disease Directors. (2008). The State of Mental Health and Aging in American Issue Brief #1: What Do the Data Tell Us? Atlanta, GA.

[17]National Alzheimer's Association. (2007). The Healthy Brain Initiative: A National Public Health Road Map to Maintaining Cognitive Health. Website: http://www.cdc.gov/aging/roadmap. Chicago, IL.

[18]Alzheimer's Research and Prevention Foundation. (2007). Daily Yoga Mediation Shown to Improve Memory, May Prevent Alzheimer's. Website: www.alzheimers prevention.org/research.htm

[19]Pagnoni, Giuseppe and Cekic, Milos. (2007). "Age effects on gray matter volume and attentional performance in Zen Meditation." Neurobiology in Aging. October. 28(10): 1623-7.

[20] AARP. (2005). Healthy Living. "Walking: Make Your Community Walkable." Website: http://www.aarp.org/health-active/walking/Articles/a2005-01-19-walking.html

[21] Walkable Communities, Inc. (1996). Glatting Jackson Kercher Anglin, Inc. 120 North Orange Avenue | Orlando, FL 32801, Toll Free: 1.866.347.2734

[22]California Newsreel. (2008). Documentary: *Unnatural Causes: Place Matters.* Episode 5, 2008. San Franciso, CA.

[23]Lorig, Sobel, Stewart, Brown, Jr., Ritter, González, Laurent, and Holman. (1999). Evidence Suggesting That a Chronic Disease Self-management Program Can Improve Health Status While Reducing Utilization and Costs: A Randomized Trial. Medical Care. 37(1):5-14. Stanford School of Medicine. Stanford Patient Education Research Center. Chronic Disease Self-management Program. Website: http://patienteducation.stanford.edu/programs/cdsmp.html.

[24]Stoppler, Melissa C. and William Shiel, Jr. (2007). "Endorphins: Natural Pain and Stress Fighters." Website: http://www.medicinenet.com/script/main/art.asp?articlekey=55001

[25]Civic Ventures. (2008). Website: www.encore.org

[26]The Penna Group. (2009). www.pennagroup.com

[27] Retirement Planning. (2009). Website: www.sunrisebeginnings.com

PENNA GROUP
L.L.C.

OUR SERVICES

Retirement Transition Life Coach:

- How prepared right now are you for a successful retirement?
- How will you replace your time after work?
- Is Re-Careering in your future?

Dreams do come true - discover your authentic self and seize a holistic life that will stimulate your mind body and spirit. Our professional coaching team will challenge you to make it happen: Learn more about
- Life Options
- Retirement Success
- ReCareer Success

SPEAKING ENGAGEMENTS

Barbara Atkins is available for speaking engagements

I hope this book will make a difference as you transition
through your phases of life!
I would like to hear from you.
PO Box 7166
Goodyear AZ 85338
www.pennagroup.com
info@pennagroup.com